CRIMCOMICS
PSYCHOSOCIAL THEORIES

KRISTA S. GEHRING
WRITER

MICHAEL R. BATISTA
ARTIST

CHERYL L. WALLACE
LETTERER

New York   Oxford
OXFORD UNIVERSITY PRESS

DEDICATION

To Vaske,
You look like Number One.

—KRISTA S. GEHRING

Dedicated to Ender,
the best doggo.

—MICHAEL R. BATISTA

FOREWORD

*Parents will realize that comic books
are not a necessary evil. I am con-
vinced that in some way or other the
democratic process will assert itself
and crime comic books will go, and
with them all they stand for and
all that sustains them* (Wertham,
1953/2012, p. 387).

Here you are, despite Fredric Wertham's
conviction that crime comics would go away,
now reading this issue of *CrimComics* as a
brief introduction to psychosocial approaches
to analyzing crime.

After World War II, psychologists, psychiatrists, and other social scientists strug-
gled to explain the postwar rise in juvenile
delinquency. In England, psychoanalyst John
Bowlby formulated *attachment theory*, con-
cluding that it was the breakdown of family
dynamics during and after the war that had
increased criminal violations by the nation's
youths (Bowlby, 1951). In America, Wertham
blamed comics (Wertham, 1954). While both
of these psychiatrists worked with juvenile
delinquents, they varied greatly in method-
ology, interpretation, and veracity (Tilley,
2012).

Over the course of the story you're about
to read, the detective characters touch upon
several of the many concepts that psychiatrists (mental health professionals who have
earned medical degrees, MDs) and psychologists (non-medical professionals who study
behavior and mental processes, holding
other doctorates such as PhDs) explore when
examining crime and courtroom processes.

Among them, they discuss Sigmund Freud's
model of personality, with its id, ego, and
superego. Even though most of us are not
Freudians, those who practiced traditional
forensic psychiatry or *psychiatric criminology* tended to be heavily Freudian in nature
for many decades. This was true of Wertham, who even met with Freud (though he
ignored Freud's advice to keep out of the
popular press) and applied psychoanalytic
principles when testifying as an expert witness in landmark cases that contributed
to insanity reform (Wertham, 1941). Con-
temporary forensic psychiatry, though, has
grown more diverse like forensic psychology,
relying less on an assumption that crime
results from acting out the id's animalistic
urges and more on findings obtained through
objective, empirical research.

Other concepts that this issue's fictional
detectives consider—from intelligence to
psychopathy—come from more meticulous
research methods, and yet each one remains
controversial because there's still something abstract about it. No one can measure
intelligence as if it were a slab of meat or wave
a meter to detect any individual's psychopathy
wavelength. Psychology is a *soft science*,
not soft in terms of degree of difficulty but
rather because its subject matter is complex
and abstract as opposed to the *hard sciences*,
which measure concrete variables such as
chemical composition of matter. People are
complex, a fact that is compounded when
studying crime because even more variables
remain unknown. The best sources of information about crimes may be the criminals

who commit them, but they are motivated to conceal facts and to misrepresent their actions even to themselves. Keep that in mind when reading how the interrogations go in this issue's investigation.

As it so happens, another figure who played an important role in the early development of forensic psychology, William Moulton Marston, has his own connection to crime comics. His mentor, Hugo Münsterberg, often called the founder of forensic psychology, studied the unreliability of eyewitness testimony and introduced Marston to the idea that psychological professionals could provide valuable assistance in legal cases as expert witnesses (Münsterberg, 1908). Seeking to advance the hard science behind their work, Marston began to measure changes in systolic blood pressure in order to detect when people are lying. Though he did not invent the polygraph, he is often called the inventor of the lie detector test for popularizing the use of physiological measures to evaluate dishonesty in criminal proceedings (Bunn, 2012). He appeared as the lie detection expert in the landmark court case that, to his frustration, led an appellate court to set the enduring legal standard that his method should *not* be admissible in court (Meyer & Weaver, 2006). Disheartened by this, yet still interested in getting the truth out of people, psychologist Marston went on to create one of the world's most famous fictional heroes, Wonder Woman, whose magic lasso could compel anyone to speak the truth. This character also happened to be one of the superheroes most heavily criticized by psychiatrist Wertham for what he perceived as a corrupting influence (Wertham, 1954).

Both Wertham and Marston saw great potential for comics to shape society through psychological means. Whereas Wertham expected the worst, Marston hoped for the best. In fact, William Moulton Marston originally got his consulting job with a comic book company because of an interview in which he praised comics for their ability to educate. Now, let's turn the page and find out what this issue of *CrimComics* has in store for educating readers today.

TRAVIS LANGLEY
Henderson State University

References

Bowlby, J. (1951). *Maternal care and mental health*. Schocken.

Bunn, G. C. (2012). *The truth machine: A social history of the lie detector*. Johns Hopkins University Press.

Meyer, R. G., & Weaver, C. M. (2006). *Law and mental health: A case-based approach*. Guilford.

Münsterberg, H. (1908). *On the witness stand: Essays on psychology and crime*. McClure.

Tilley, C. L. (2012). Seducing the innocent: Fredric Wertham and the falsifications that helped condemn comics. *Information & Culture: A Journal of History, 47*(4), 383–413.

Wertham, F. (1941). *Dark legend: A study in murder*. Duell, Sloan, & Pearce.

Wertham, F. (1953/2012). Fredric Wertham, crusader against comics, makes his case to parents. In K. Franz & S. Smulyan (Eds.), *Major problems in American popular culture: Documents and essays* (pp. 383–387). Wadsworth.

Wertham, F. (1954). *Seduction of the innocent*. Kennikat.

PREFACE

Readers of the *CrimComics* series will notice that this issue is a little different from the previous ones. Instead of creating a narrative about theories that are within a socihistorical context, I decided to introduce various concepts found in the psychology discipline by embedding them in a criminal investigation scenario. Readers should note that this narrative is completely fictional and intended only to be a vehicle to discuss these concepts. It is also an homage to all of the crime television shows and movies, both true and fictional, which I imagine a lot of our readers enjoy watching.

Due to its interdisciplinary nature, the field of criminology has borrowed from many other disciplines to help explain criminal behavior. One discipline in particular that has been especially helpful in explaining behavior has been psychology. For example, in *CrimComics*: *Social Learning Theories* it was illustrated how Robert Burgess and Ronald Akers used ideas from psychologists B. F. Skinner and Albert Bandura to develop social learning theory.

The same can be said for the concepts presented in this issue, as here we will cover additional psychological concepts and how they are related to crime. Indeed, many of these concepts were not initially developed to explain crime, but criminology has later used them to do so. For example, intelligence tests were first developed in Europe and America in the early 1900s in order to objectively measure a person's cognitive ability. The French government commissioned French psychologist Alfred Binet to develop a test that could identify students who might have the most difficulty in school. In 1905, Binet, with his colleague Theodore Simon, created the Binet-Simon Scale, which became the basis for modern intelligence testing. When the Binet-Simon Scale was brought to the United States, Stanford psychologist Lewis Terman standardized it on a sample of American participants. This adapted test was named the Stanford-Binet Scale and has been the standard intelligence test used in the United States. This scale reduced the score to one number that represented the individual's intelligence quotient, or IQ. This test was then later used with criminal justice populations to determine if there was a relationship between IQ and crime or a difference between the IQs of offenders and non-offenders. So, while this concept was not originally developed to explain criminal behavior, scholars have used it to do so.

The same can be said for the concept of personality. There are many, many scholars who have taken on the task of explaining and parsing out the various components that we collectively call "personality." These individuals include Carl Jung, Sigmund Freud, Erik Erikson, Hans Eysenck, Carl Rogers, and Abraham Maslow, to name a few. Furthermore, these scholars do not agree on how personality is developed and shaped, or what its components are. However, the notion of personality—that it is a relatively enduring, distinctive, and functional psychological characteristics that results from an individual's temperament interacting with his or her cultural and developmental experiences—is the framework from which these scholars based their ideas on. Again, these ideas were originally developed to explain everyone's personality; however, criminologists used these ideas about personality to explain the personalities of individuals who engaged in crime.

Hopefully, these paragraphs have illustrated that the concepts of IQ and personality have an extensive and rich historical development, far too lengthy to cover in the pages of this volume. However, we would encourage readers to explore these concepts further if this has piqued their interest, as these psychological concepts and theories have fascinating histories. For now, readers will enjoy their introduction and explanation in the criminal investigation narrative involving Detectives Zuniga and Acosta. Perhaps once *CrimComics* is complete, there will be a *PsyComics* . . .

As with any book project, *CrimComics* consumed much time and effort, perhaps more so than a traditional textbook. Thinking about theory—and, in particular, trying to design a work that best conveys the theories in a visual medium—is fun. Still, with busy lives, finding the space in one's day to carefully research, write, illustrate, ink, and letter the pages of this work is a source of some stress. We were fortunate, however, to have had an amazing amount of support during these times from family, friends, and Oxford University Press. We also want to acknowledge the talents of Cheryl Wallace. Cheryl's flair for lettering allowed us to get our ideas across to the readers.

The support of these and so many other individuals has made creating *CrimComics* possible and a rewarding experience for us. We would like to thank the following reviewers: Viviana Andreescu, University of Louisville; Thomas Chuda, Bunker Hill Community College; Ellen G. Cohn, Florida International University; Anthony W. Flores, California State University, Bakersfield; Robert Jenkot, Coastal Carolina University; Suman Kakar, Florida International University; Elizabeth B. Perkins, Morehead State University; and, Robert Hare, University of British Columbia. We hope that this and other issues of *CrimComics* will inspire in your students a passion to learn criminological theory.

Psychosocial Theories

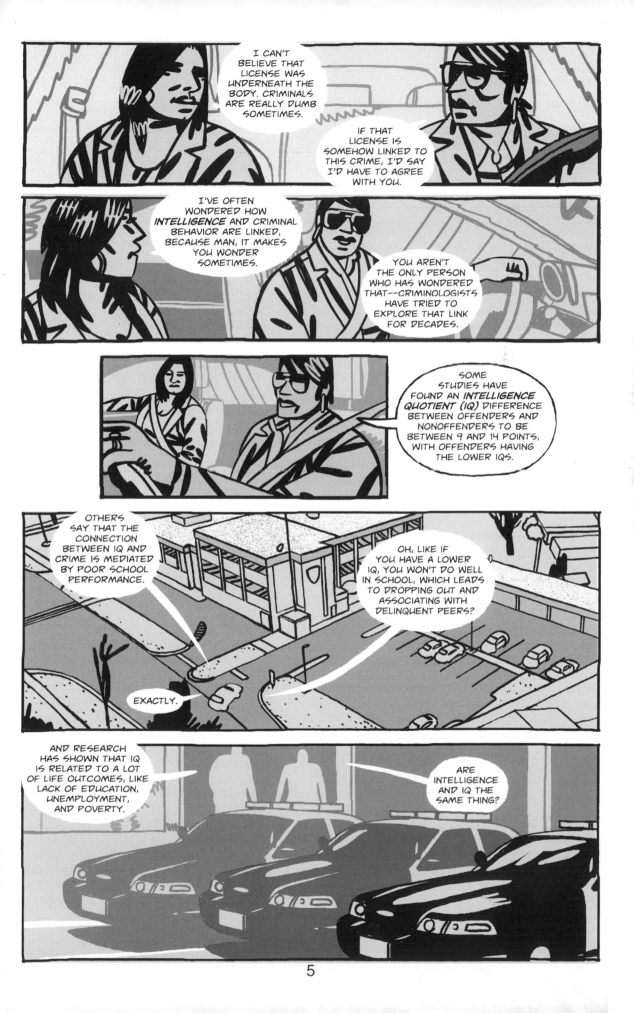

Personality Traits Positively Linked to Criminal Behavior

Negative emotionality: Tendency to interpret situations as aversive and to react to them with irritation and anger.

"I WAS GETTING A DRINK AT MY REGULAR PLACE, YOU KNOW, MINDING MY OWN BUSINESS. THIS GUY IS STARING AT ME."

"I WAS THIS CLOSE TO GETTING UP AND PUNCHING HIM IN THE FACE, FOR STARING, YOU KNOW..."

"...BUT THE GUY ACTUALLY COMES OVER TO ME, AND WE GET TO TALKING. WE TALK FOR A WHILE, ACTUALLY. AND THEN HE ASKS ME IF I'D BE INTERESTED IN MAKING A LOT OF MONEY."

"I TOLD HIM SURE, WHAT ARE WE TALKING ABOUT?"

Impulsiveness: Trait most linked to criminal behavior. Tendency to act without giving much thought to the consequences of actions.

"HE TOLD ME HE NEEDED HIS WIFE DEAD. DIDN'T TELL ME WHY, AND I DIDN'T ASK."

"HE SAID HE'D PAY ME $50,000 TO DO IT."

"I THOUGHT ABOUT IT FOR MAYBE A SECOND, AND THEN I SAID OKAY."

Sensation seeking: Desire for exciting, new, and risky sensations and experiences. It's tied to impulsiveness and fearlessness.

"I MEAN, I'VE NEVER DONE ANYTHING LIKE THIS BEFORE. THE THOUGHT OF IT, I'LL ADMIT, WAS KIND OF EXCITING."

"I WAS GOING TO BE, LIKE, A HITMAN OR SOMETHING."

"AND FIFTY GRAND? THAT WAS A LOT OF MONEY."

Personality Traits Negatively Linked to Criminal Behavior

Empathy: The ability to understand the feelings and distress of others and "feel what they feel." Thompson obviously couldn't care less—he had little empathy for Nancy.

"I WENT TO THE HOUSE AND PRETENDED I WAS DELIVERING FLOWERS. WHEN SHE OPENED THE DOOR, I POINTED A GUN AT HER FACE."

"SHE SCREAMED AND RAN, BUT I SHOT HER IN THE DINING ROOM."

Altruism: The action component of empathy, such as active concern for others. Not present in the current narrative.

"I KNEW I NEEDED TO GET OUT OF THERE FAST, SO I WRAPPED HER UP IN THE AREA RUG THAT SHE FELL ON."

"THAT WAS ACTUALLY PRETTY CONVENIENT, BECAUSE IT WAS A GREAT WAY TO GET HER OUT OF THE HOUSE."

Conscientiousness: Being well-organized, disciplined, and responsible. The opposite is being unreliable, careless, irresponsible, and unscrupulous.

"HONESTLY, I HADN'T THOUGHT THAT MUCH ABOUT WHAT I WAS GOING TO DO WITH THE BODY."

"I WAS JUST MAKING IT UP AS I WENT AT THAT POINT."

Agreeableness: Tendency to be friendly, considerate, helpful, and cooperative with others. The opposite is hostility, suspicion of others, unfriendliness, and lacking empathy.

"SINCE I HADN'T PLANNED THINGS THAT FAR, I THOUGHT I'D JUST DUMP IT ON THE SIDE OF THE ROAD."

"BUT THEN THIS 'GOOD SAMARITAN' STOPPED TO SEE IF I NEEDED HELP."

"I CUSSED HIM OUT AND RAN HIM OFF."

IS THIS THE SAME AS *ANTISOCIAL PERSONALITY DISORDER (ASPD)?*

PAYING ATTENTION IN ALL THOSE COLLEGE PSYCHOLOGY CLASSES COMES IN HANDY WITH THIS JOB.

I CAN SEE THAT!

KIND OF, BUT NOT REALLY-- ASPD IS A CLINICAL DIAGNOSIS FOUND IN THE *DSM-5,** A PUBLICATION USED TO CLASSIFY MENTAL DISORDERS.

THE ASPD DIAGNOSIS REALLY ONLY FOCUSES ON BEHAVIOR. PSYCHOPATHY NOT ONLY HAS BEHAVIOR TRAITS, BUT THERE IS THAT INTERPERSONAL/ AFFECTIVE COMPONENT AS WELL.

I THINK IT'S IMPORTANT TO KNOW BECAUSE SO MANY PEOPLE THINK THAT A LOT OF INDIVIDUALS WHO COMMIT CRIME HAVE A *MENTAL ILLNESS.*

I READ A STUDY THAT LOOKED AT CRIMES COMMITTED BY PEOPLE WITH SERIOUS MENTAL DISORDERS, AND IT FOUND THAT ONLY 7.5% OF THE CRIMES WERE DIRECTLY RELATED TO SYMPTOMS OF MENTAL ILLNESS.

BUT, A LOT OF PEOPLE WHO ARE MENTALLY ILL ARE IN THE CRIMINAL JUSTICE SYSTEM THANKS TO *DEINSTITUTION- ALIZATION.*

FOR EXAMPLE, APPROXIMATELY 20% OF INMATES IN JAILS AND 15% OF INMATES IN STATE PRISONS HAVE A SERIOUS MENTAL ILLNESS.

*DIAGNOSTIC AND STATISTICAL MANUAL OF MENTAL DISORDERS, FIFTH EDITION.

23

*ANTISOCIAL PERSONALITY IS ONE OF THE BIG FOUR RISK FACTORS FOR CRIMINAL BEHAVIOR.

THE NARRATIVE IN THIS ISSUE WAS USED TO INTRODUCE THE READER TO MANY CONCEPTS RELATED TO PSYCHOSOCIAL THEORIES OF CRIME. IT BEGAN WITH A DISCUSSION OF INTELLIGENCE AND THE IQ-CRIME CONNECTION. INTELLIGENCE IS OUR GLOBAL CAPACITY TO ACT PURPOSEFULLY, TO THINK RATIONALLY, AND TO EFFECTIVELY DEAL WITH OUR ENVIRONMENT. THE INTELLIGENCE QUOTIENT, OR IQ, IS OUR ATTEMPT TO MEASURE INTELLIGENCE. SOME STUDIES HAVE FOUND AN IQ DIFFERENCE BETWEEN OFFENDERS AND NONOFFENDERS TO BE BETWEEN 9 AND 14 POINTS, WITH OFFENDERS HAVING THE LOWER IQS. HOWEVER, MOST SCHOLARS BELIEVE THE CONNECTION BETWEEN IQ AND CRIME IS MEDIATED BY POOR SCHOOL PERFORMANCE. IN ORDER TO PREVENT CRIME USING THIS CONCEPT, PROGRAMS SHOULD BE IMPLEMENTED THAT PROMOTE POSITIVE SCHOOL EXPERIENCES FOR INDIVIDUALS WITH LOWER IQS.

TEMPERAMENT AND PERSONALITY HAVE ALSO BEEN LINKED TO CRIMINAL BEHAVIOR. A BROAD THEORY OF PERSONALITY WAS INTRODUCED BY SIGMUND FREUD THAT CONSISTED OF THE ID, EGO, AND SUPEREGO INTERACTING WITH EACH OTHER. WHILE FREUD DID NOT DISCUSS HOW PERSONALITY WAS LINKED TO CRIME, HIS IDEAS INSPIRED CRIMINOLOGISTS TO DO SO. THERE ARE MANY PERSONALITY TRAITS THAT ARE POSITIVELY AND NEGATIVELY RELATED TO CRIMINAL BEHAVIOR, INCLUDING NEGATIVE EMOTIONALITY, IMPULSIVENESS, SENSATION SEEKING, EMPATHY, ALTRUISM, CONSCIENTIOUSNESS, AND AGREEABLENESS. RESEARCH HAS FOUND THAT ANTISOCIAL PERSONALITY IS A RISK FACTOR FOR CRIMINAL BEHAVIOR, AND COGNITIVE BEHAVIORAL PROGRAMS THAT TARGET IMPULSIVITY, NEGATIVE EMOTIONALITY, AND RISK-TAKING BEHAVIOR MAY LEAD TO IMPROVED OUTCOMES.

PSYCHOPATHY IS A SYNDROME CHARACTERIZED BY A PERSON'S INABILITY TO TIE SOCIAL EMOTIONS TO COGNITIONS. HERVEY CLECKLEY WAS ONE OF THE FIRST SCHOLARS TO EXPLORE PSYCHOPATHY AND STATE THAT THESE INDIVIDUALS ARE INTELLIGENT, SELF-CENTERED, GLIB, SUPERFICIALLY CHARMING, AND A WHOLE HOST OF OTHER CHARACTERISTICS. ROBERT HARE BUILT UPON CLECKLEY'S IDEAS ABOUT PSYCHOPATHY AND DEVELOPED THE PSYCHOPATHY CHECKLIST-REVISED (PCL-R). THIS IS A PSYCHOLOGICAL ASSESSMENT TOOL COMMONLY USED TO ASSESS THE PRESENCE OF PSYCHOPATHY IN INDIVIDUALS. THE BEHAVIOR OF PSYCHOPATHS, OFTEN REFERRED TO AS PRIMARY PSYCHOPATHS, HAS A BIOLOGICAL BASIS. ON THE OTHER HAND, SOCIOPATHS, ALSO KNOWN AS SECONDARY PSYCHOPATHS, EXHIBIT SIMILAR BEHAVIORS, BUT THE ETIOLOGY OF THE BEHAVIOR IS DIFFERENT. THESE INDIVIDUALS' BEHAVIOR IS DUE TO AN ADAPTATION TO SOME SEVERE TRAUMA IN EARLY LIFE OR POOR PARENTING. COGNITIVE BEHAVIORAL TREATMENT MAY BE USED TO ADDRESS PSYCHOPATHY, BUT PSYCHOPATHS ARE DIFFICULT TO TREAT.

MENTAL ILLNESS IS ALSO AN ISSUE THAT IS DISCUSSED REGARDING JUSTICE-INVOLVED INDIVIDUALS. HOWEVER, VERY FEW CRIMES ARE DIRECTLY RELATED TO SYMPTOMS OF MENTAL ILLNESS. THE REASON SO MANY INDIVIDUALS WHO HAVE MENTAL ILLNESS ARE IN THE CRIMINAL JUSTICE SYSTEM IS DUE TO THE DEINSTITUTIONALIZATION MOVEMENT. IT IS POSSIBLE THAT THESE INDIVIDUALS WOULD BE BETTER SERVED BY TREATING THIS AS A PUBLIC HEALTH PROBLEM, NOT A CRIMINAL JUSTICE ISSUE.

Key Terms

Psychosocial Theories
Intelligence
Intelligence Quotient (IQ)
Sigmund Freud
Psychoanalysis
Ego
Id
Superego
Personality
Temperament
Negative Emotionality
Impulsiveness
Sensation Seeking
Empathy
Altruism
Conscientiousness
Agreeableness
Psychopath
Hervey Cleckley
Psychopathy
Robert Hare
Psychology Checklist-Revised (PCL-R)
Social Emotions
Primary Psychopaths
Amygdala

Prefrontal Cortex
Sociopaths
Secondary Psychopaths
Antisocial Personality Disorder (ASPD)
Mental Illness
Deinstitutionalization
Antisocial Personality

Discussion Questions

1. Describe the relationship between crime and IQ. What does the research show regarding this relationship? Why is this topic controversial?

2. Describe in detail the relationship that has been found between personality and crime. What are the policy implications of this perspective?

3. How are the amygdala and prefrontal cortex related to behavior? How might this explain the behavior of psychopaths?

4. Describe the difference between primary and secondary psychopaths. Which etiology do you believe explains their behavior the best (i.e., biological basis or environmental influences), and why?

5. Describe deinstitutionalization. How did this impact the criminal justice system?

Suggested Readings

Agnew, R., Brezina, T., Wright, J. P., & Cullen, F. T. (2002). Strain, personality traits, and delinquency: Extending general strain theory. *Criminology*, 40, 43–71.

Caspi, A., Moffitt, T. E., Silva, P. A., Loeber, M. S., Krueger, R. F., & Schmutte, P. S. (1994). Are some people crime prone? Replications of the personality crime relationship across countries, genders, races, and methods. *Criminology*, 32, 163–196.

Cleckley, H. (1941). *The mask of sanity*. C.V. Mosby Company.

Hare, R. D. (1999). *Without conscience: The disturbing world of the psychopaths among us*. The Guilford Press.

Hare, R. D. (2003). *Manual for the Revised Psychopathy Checklist* (2nd ed.). Multi-Health Systems.

Lykken, D. (1995). *The antisocial personalities*. Lawrence Erlbaum Associates.